ICNC **SPECIAL REPORT** SERIES

How to Win Well

Civil Resistance Breakthroughs and the Path to Democracy

Jonathan Pinckney

Table of Contents

Introduction 1

How Nonviolent Uprisings Succeed 5

The Effects of the Breakthrough Types 8

Testing the Influence of Civil Resistance-Initiated Breakthroughs on Democratization . . . 10

Breakthrough by Elections in the 2018 Armenian Velvet Revolution 14

Breakthrough by Coup d'État in the 2011 Egyptian Revolution 16

Takeaways and Recommendations 19

References 21

Appendix 25
    Coding Rules for Determining Breakthrough Type 25
    Example Breakthrough Type Coding Determinations 26
    TABLE A1: Complete List of Cases with Breakthrough Types 28
    TABLE A2: Full OLS Model Regression Table and Robustness Check Results 30

About the Author 32

Figures

FIGURE 1: Pathways from Civil Resistance to a New Regime 9

FIGURE 2: Incidence of the Civil Resistance Breakthrough Types from 1945 to 2011 . . . 11

FIGURE 3: Average Levels of Democracy Across Different Breakthroughs 12

FIGURE 4: Effects of Elections/Negotiations on Democracy
Five Years After Breakthrough 13

FIGURE A1: Primary Model Robustness Checks (t + 1 to t + 10) 31

INTRODUCTION

ON APRIL 11, 2019, after four months of citizen-led nonviolent protests, Sudan's military announced that they had deposed dictatorial President Omar al-Bashir and placed him under house arrest. The protesters, led by the Sudanese Professionals Association (SPA), rejoiced that the dictator was gone but expressed caution at how he had been removed. Protesters stayed on the streets, demanding not just the removal of Bashir but a more comprehensive overhaul of the regime that had supported him, including the military leaders who had overthrown him.[1]

Their caution was warranted. Large nonviolent resistance movements have been one of the central forces for political transformation of dictatorships in recent history (Ackerman and DuVall 2000; Chenoweth and Stephan 2011; Nepstad 2011). Numerous studies have also shown that when dictators are ousted through peaceful protests like those in Sudan, their ouster is much more likely to lead to democracy (Bayer, Bethke, and Lambach 2016; Bethke and Pinckney 2019; Celestino and Gleditsch 2013; Karatnycky and Ackerman 2005; Pinckney 2018). Yet many of these hopeful moments of nonviolent change, far from ushering in democracy, have instead witnessed emergent regimes just as autocratic as, or even worse than, the ones that preceded them.

Sudan's own history bears witness to these sad realities. Twice since Sudanese independence mass uprisings have brought down entrenched Sudanese dictators: first in 1965 when student-initiated protests led to the ouster of President Ibrahim Abboud, and then in 1985 when a general strike brought down President Jaafar Nimeiry (Abdulshafi 2019). In both cases the dictator's downfall led to brief periods of democratization. However, the entrenched power of anti-democratic elites—particularly the military—brought the country back to a dictatorship. Removing a dictator from power, even through nonviolent resistance, was not enough to ensure democratic change.

---

1 For more information, please see the ICNC publication *Sudan's 2019 Revolution: The Power of Civil Resistance* by Dr. Stephen Zunes. This study contains interviews with activists and civil society groups that led the movement as well as with journalists and scholars who chronicled the struggle.

This special report addresses the crucial time after a civil resistance movement has achieved a political breakthrough against a dictator. The key questions it looks to answer are these:

- What are the ways in which civil resistance movements achieve political breakthroughs to oust entrenched dictators?
- Which civil resistance-initiated breakthroughs tend to put countries on a pathway to democracy?
- What can external actors do to help movements increase their chances for more successful democratic breakthrough and transition?

Research into nonviolent resistance and democratization points to a few key factors in answering these questions. First, when uprisings are nonviolent, they are more likely to lead to democracy (Celestino and Gleditsch 2013; Chenoweth and Stephan 2011; Karatnycky and Ackerman 2005). Additionally, research indicates that political dynamics during the period of transition have critical long-term consequences (Fernandes 2015). Enduring social mobilization and civic mobilization that strengthen new institutions are crucial for democratization (Pinckney 2018). Yet it is not clear how these positive patterns of pro-democracy mobilization can be brought about or supported.

The report addresses this gap by building on Pinckney's (2014) categorization of civil resistance "breakthrough types,"[2] which identifies the six ways in which civil resistance campaigns have achieved major political breakthroughs against non-democratic regimes in the post–World War II period, such as roundtable negotiations, elections, or military coups.

The report's key argument is that the type of breakthrough critically shapes the political transition that follows it, pushing the transition in either a democratic or undemocratic direction. This occurs because the breakthrough types differ along three key dimensions:

1. the relative power balance between the incumbent regime and opposition actors;
2. the type of actor which takes initiative at the beginning of the transition (as well as the type of initiative the actor takes); and
3. the degree of institutionalization of the transition process.

The movements leading to democracy are those that begin with breakthroughs characterized by a power balance favorable to a nonviolent *challenger,* an *opposition-driven initiative,* and *institutional channels. Negotiations* and *elections* are the breakthroughs

---

2 Pinckney (2014) refers to these as "mechanisms of success." I use the term "breakthrough" here to emphasize that these are moments of significant change, but do not necessarily lead automatically to long-term success.

that best approximate these three characteristics and thus are expected to lead to more democratic outcomes.

The report tests whether this expectation holds true by statistically examining detailed information on 76 transitions initiated by civil resistance campaigns from 1945 through 2011. The findings of this analysis support the report's expectations. The report then illustrates the impact of different breakthroughs on transitional trajectories through a brief examination of two case studies: the 2018 Velvet Revolution in Armenia and the 2011 Arab Spring in Egypt.

Finally, based on its findings, the report offers specific recommendations to practitioners and policymakers interested in positively influencing the democratic trajectories of nonviolent uprisings. In particular, it recommends that the external allies of nonviolent movements and those on the ground who spearhead civil resistance:

- build movements' capacities to bring about, own, and utilize a democratizing breakthrough to advance movements' goals and democratic transitions;
- use civil resistance-initiated breakthroughs to put democratizers in positions of political influence;
- establish new institutional avenues of action and political participation; and
- approach political involvement of the military with significant skepticism and care.

How Nonviolent Uprisings Succeed

Mass uprisings that have primarily relied on nonviolent tactics to achieve political change, are one of the most powerful forces for political transition today. Chenoweth and Stephan (2011) identify over one hundred nonviolent resistance movements between 1900 and 2006 which sought to oust undemocratic regimes, end military occupations, or create new states. The Global Nonviolent Action Database (Lakey 2011), which collects data on all kinds of nonviolent uprisings, has identified more than one thousand campaigns of primarily nonviolent action with a wide variety of goals and tactics.

The power of nonviolent uprisings comes primarily from their superior ability—on average, eleven times greater—relative to violent uprisings to attract mass participation (Chenoweth and Stephan 2011), and, through this, to gain points of "leverage" (Schock 2005) and undermine autocratic regimes' "pillars of support" (Helvey 2004). In particular, nonviolent resistance movements often undermine the loyalty of the military or other security forces to the regime (Nepstad 2011). The underlying logic of civil resistance rests on an insight from social and political theorists and practitioners of nonviolent action, described in detail by Gene Sharp (1973, 2005), that power systems rely on the cooperation of their subjects. When enough ordinary people refuse to cooperate, the system breaks down.

This simple strategic logic, however, tells us little about the ways in which primarily nonviolent uprisings bring about real political change. In democracies, protest can lead to change by shifting public opinion or voting behavior (Madestam et al. 2013; Wasow 2017). But how do nonviolent campaigns move from the streets to the corridors of power when autocratic political systems do not provide such avenues?

Pinckney (2014) offers one answer to this question by developing an empirical categorization of six key breakthrough mechanisms through which pressure by a nonviolent resistance campaign leads to a significant change in the incumbent regime. Because they challenge the power of those in authority, breakthroughs necessarily initiate a process of political transition as players in the political game seek to establish a new set of rules. The six distinctive types of breakthrough,[3] roughly arranged from least to most confrontational, are:

---

3   The types of breakthrough are derived from a careful observation of the dynamics of civil resistance campaigns in the post–World War II period and are defined empirically rather than theoretically. The six breakthrough types are not strictly based on theory, but rather are a way of easily distinguishing the different nonviolent uprisings that have successfully achieved a major political breakthrough and initiated a process of political transition. The primary goal of such categorization is to include all relevant breakthrough cases as observed in real-life nonviolent revolutions. These categories differ from Gene Sharp's (2005) concept of "mechanisms of change" (such as conversion, accommodation, coercion, and disintegration) which draws on his underlying theory of power and does not concern itself with transition processes that might follow.

1. National negotiation between the opposition and the undemocratic regime

The first breakthrough type is a *negotiation*. In these breakthroughs the civil resistance campaign engages in a bargaining process with the regime (often mediated by domestic or international third parties) to establish the terms of a possible transitional power-sharing arrangement and the eventual departure of the regime. Negotiations are only considered to be a breakthrough if they result in the achievement of the central goal of the pro-democracy campaign.[4]

2. Competitive national election

The second breakthrough type is an *election*, in which the campaign achieves its goal through an institutionalized electoral process. Typically, this occurs through the electoral victory of a relatively united opposition over the incumbent regime. Since these campaigns take place in countries without regular free and fair democratic elections, nonviolent resistance is often necessary, both to pressure the incumbent regime to hold the election and to ensure that the regime honors the election outcome. Some of the best examples of this mechanism are the "Color Revolutions" of the early 2000s (Bunce and Wolchik 2011).

3. Resignation of the head of the undemocratic regime

The third breakthrough type is *resignation*, in which the regime relinquishes power independent of an election, negotiation, or other previously institutionalized or negotiated processes due to the ongoing pressure from a civil resistance campaign. The leaders of the regime, perhaps fearing the consequences of remaining in power, choose to step down from power. For example, this was the breakthrough type in the East German revolution in 1989, as a string of resignations by members of the Communist Party led to the collapse of the regime (Nepstad 2011).

4. External interventions

The fourth breakthrough type is an *external intervention*, in which direct actions by an external actor bring about regime change in response to the ongoing civil resistance campaign. Interventions may be diplomatic (as in the Ruhrkampf in 1923) or military (as in East Timor in 1999). The key distinguishing factor of an intervention as a breakthrough type is that the intervention precipitates the achievement of the nonviolent campaign's goal and is a necessary component of its success.

---

4 Negotiations, often with external mediation, take place throughout many civil resistance campaigns even if they do not directly lead to that campaign's final outcome. This special report is only examining negotiations that directly lead to the breakdown of an opponent regime. For more on the general role of negotiations in civil resistance see Dudouet 2008, Svensson and Lundgren 2018 and Wanis-St. John and Rosen 2017.

5. Coups d'état (violent or peaceful)

The fifth breakthrough type is a *coup d'état*, in which a group of regime elites independently seizes power. A coup may take the classic form of a military takeover with soldiers in the streets or may take place behind closed doors in the corridors of power. While coups are typically initiated without the knowledge of the civil resistance campaign, the opening for coups is often created by a civil resistance campaign. The campaign creates a crisis-packed situation for an incumbent regime or its head, weakening its authority and, in turn, giving other organized actors an opportunity to assert their influence and seize political power.

6. Overwhelming the undemocratic regime

Finally, the most dramatic breakthrough type in civil resistance struggles is *overwhelming*. An overwhelming is the closest empirical approximation to what Gene Sharp described as "disintegration" (Sharp 2005). In this breakthrough, participation in the civil resistance campaign reaches such a high level, and defection from the regime becomes so widespread, that the organs of government cease to function and the regime collapses. For instance, in the 2005 Tulip Revolution in Kyrgyzstan, the police stopped repressing the increasingly massive protests, and protesters continued occupation of the major government buildings in Bishkek, resulting in authoritarian president Askar Akayev fleeing the country without formally renouncing power.[5]

These six identified breakthrough types are an observational categorization, derived from examining all the cases in which civil resistance in a non-democracy led to a change in political regime from 1945 until 2011. Other breakthroughs in civil resistance struggles are theoretically possible but have not yet occurred. These identified categories provide a meaningful way to distinguish breakthroughs that is both simple to apply and inclusive of all actual cases in recent history.

These kinds of breakthrough (and others) can also happen outside of the context of civil resistance, and there are various schemes in academic literature for categorizing them.[6] It is beyond the scope of this report to examine the effects of different breakthroughs across all non-democratic regime contexts outside of civil resistance struggles. Consequently, this report focuses on the impact of the identified breakthroughs in the context of a civil resistance movement.

---

[5] Akayev did eventually formally resign from power, but the resignation only took place after his regime had lost power. Thus, in this case the formal resignation was not the breakthrough mechanism because it took place after the critical shift in power had already occurred.

[6] For example, see Geddes, Wright, and Frantz 2014.

The Effects of the Breakthrough Types

Ending an autocratic regime is only the first step in the political transformation process. Political transitions involve many steps before a new regime can be established (O'Donnell and Schmitter 1986). Thus, breakthrough types do not immediately set a country's long-term political trajectory in stone. Founding elections, even if free and fair, do not necessarily lead to full-fledged democracy.

However, the means of breaking through into a political transition can significantly influence how the political transition develops, and thus influence the shape of the new regime at the transition's end.[7] This is in part because nonviolent resistance campaigns typically have their greatest political influence at the moment when an old regime breaks down. Once a political transition has begun it can be difficult to maintain popular mobilization, and old political elites may reassert themselves and return to wielding political power (Pinckney 2018).

Breakthrough types differ in their impact on transitions because they vary along three dimensions:

1. How a breakthrough affects the balance of power between new political challengers and old political elites;
2. Which actor assumes initiative for the transition; and
3. The degree to which the breakthrough follows institutional avenues of action.

Both the balance of power and the actor that wields political initiative help determine whose preferences will shape the political decisions made during the transition. If the way in which the old regime was ousted places most of the levers of political power and the initiative for making important transitional decisions in the hands of old regime elites, then it is likely that less democratic preferences will prevail. In contrast, if the type of breakthrough puts significant resources for political influence in the hands of new political challengers, it is more likely (though certainly not guaranteed) that a more democratic political system may emerge.

Institutionalization of the breakthrough guards against the possibility that transitions will turn into winner-take-all struggles for political influence and helps establish a new regime built upon the rule of law with effective institutional constraints. This can help avoid "street

---

[7] It is important to note that civil resistance campaign actions or structures may make some breakthrough types more likely than others. For instance, highly diffuse, non-hierarchical movements will likely struggle to negotiate with an autocratic regime, and thus may have this means of breakthrough closed off. Other campaigns may build internal democratic structures that prefigure democratic politics, facilitating participation in elections. We know little about the campaign characteristics that cross-nationally facilitate certain breakthrough types, and it is beyond the scope of this report to examine this question, but see important work from other scholars on the subject in Butcher, Gray, and Mitchell 2018 or Nepstad 2015.

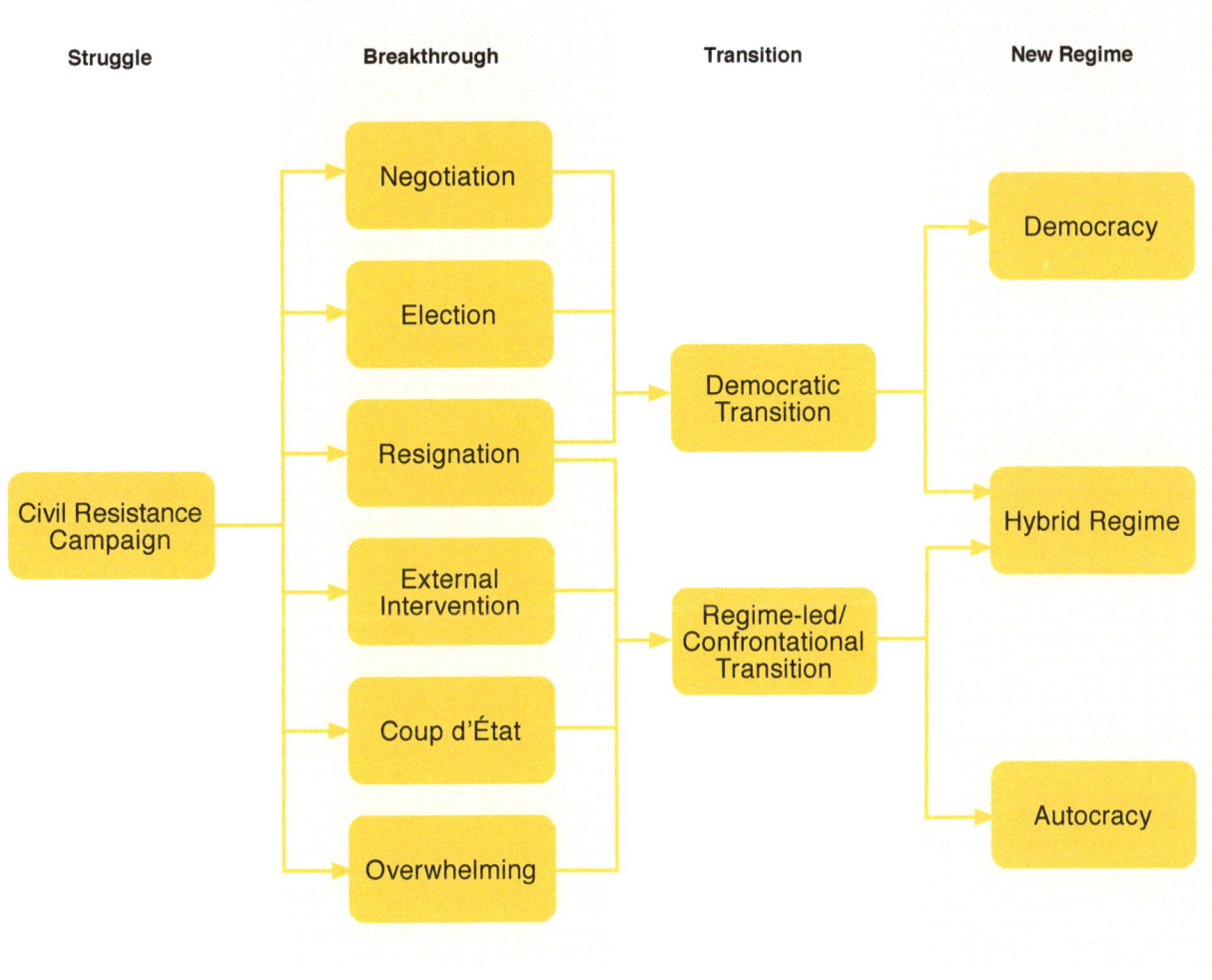

FIGURE 1: Pathways from Civil Resistance to a New Regime

Source: Created by the author

radicalism," identified as one of the major challenges faced by nonviolent resistance movements during transitions to democracy (Pinckney 2018).

The above characteristics for each of the six breakthrough types can have significant effects on the political dynamics during the transition period that follows them. These dynamics, in turn, can have a strong influence on the type of regime (democracy, hybrid or autocracy) that follows the political transition.

Figure 1 lists the six breakthroughs described earlier in the report with the expected transition outcomes following the successful ousting of non-democratic regimes. The breakthrough mechanisms that best incorporate the positive characteristics of (1) a favorable balance of power; (2) right actor taking initiative; and (3) a degree of institutionalization are negotiations and elections.

This report assumes these specific breakthroughs will tend to lead to more cooperative transitions that will be more likely to end in democracy. For the most part, transitions initiated through external intervention, a coup, or overwhelming do not have these positive characteristics and thus will be more likely to lead to what this report refers to as a regime-led or confrontational transition, which is more likely to end in a new autocracy. Transitions initiated through resignations are in a medial category, sometimes leading to more cooperative transitions and sometimes leading to more confrontational transitions.

No breakthrough type is a guarantee of democratic success. Nor does any breakthrough type fully determine democratic failure. Establishing democracy, particularly a strong democracy with liberal values and the protection of human rights, is always an uncertain enterprise. The argument here is that civil resistance-initiated breakthrough types consistently influence a transition toward or away from democracy; some of the specific breakthroughs push more toward democracy and others away from democracy, as illustrated in **Figure 1**.

Testing the Influence of Civil Resistance-Initiated Breakthroughs on Democratization

How well does the argument laid out in **Figure 1** map onto actual political transitions? This section analyzes 76 transitions brought about primarily through nonviolent resistance from 1945-2011 (Pinckney 2018) and maps the identified six breakthroughs onto them. The information about civil resistance campaigns comes primarily from NAVCO 1.1 (Stephan and Chenoweth 2008), NAVCO 2.0 (Chenoweth and Lewis 2013), and the Global Nonviolent Action Database (Lakey 2011). When these sources did not provide enough information to identify a specific civil resistance-initiated breakthrough, secondary sources specific to the case were consulted.

Cases were classified based on which of the breakthroughs were the most important and immediate cause of regime change. The categorization of a case into one of these categories does not imply that aspects of the other breakthrough types did not occur. For instance, negotiations between a campaign and regime frequently occur during the campaign's period of struggle without leading to a breakthrough. A case would only be considered to have had negotiations as its breakthrough type if the negotiations led directly to the end of the old regime and initiation of a political transition, for instance through directly bringing about the establishment of temporary power-sharing arrangements.[8]

---

8 More discussion of these coding rules can be found in the appendix.

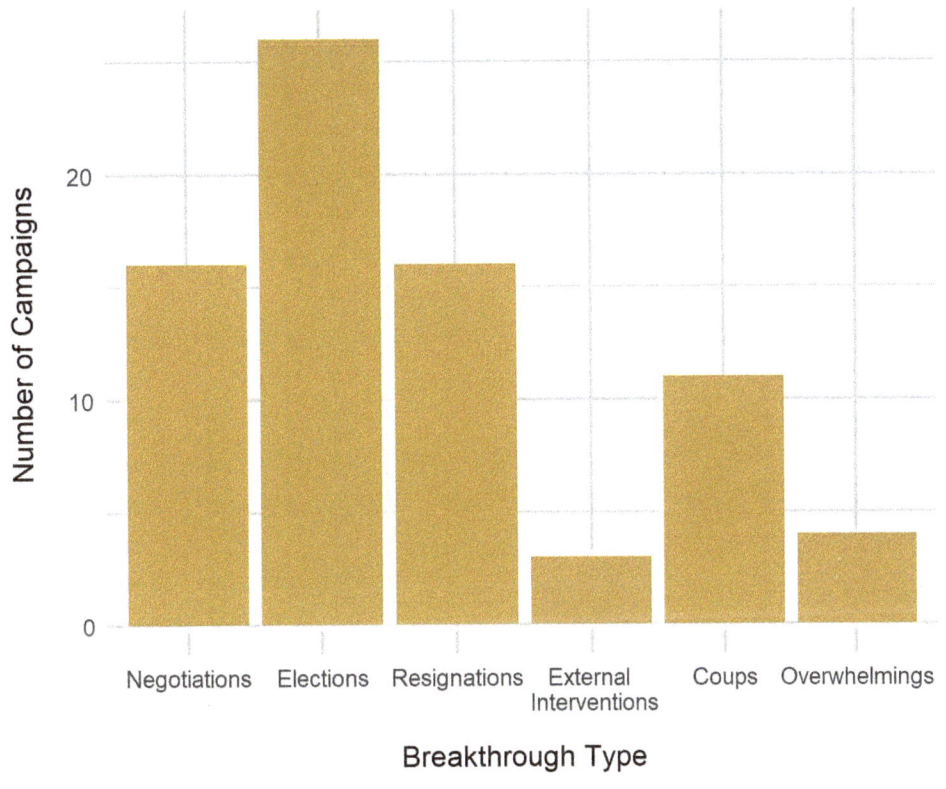

FIGURE 2: Incidence of the Civil Resistance Breakthrough Types from 1945 to 2011
Source: Author calculation based on NAVCO dataset and original data collection

Figure 2 shows the distribution of breakthroughs across the civil resistance-induced transitions. The most common of the six breakthroughs in successful civil resistance campaigns have been elections, occurring in 26 cases. The rarest breakthroughs are external interventions, with only three cases, and overwhelmings, with only four cases.

The relative rarity of some of these breakthroughs makes it impossible to analyze each type of breakthrough individually using standard statistical methods. Thus, the remainder of this section combines negotiations and elections—the breakthroughs expected to have the strongest positive effects on democracy—and contrasts them with the four other types of breakthrough.

The first finding from making this contrast is that breakthroughs have a strong impact on the average levels of democracy over time. **Figure 3** shows the average levels of democracy before and after a successful civil resistance campaign in countries whose transition was initiated through a negotiation or election as compared to the other four breakthroughs. A dashed vertical line indicates the breakthrough year. Democracy is measured using the Polyarchy score from the Varieties of Democracy project (Coppedge et al. 2018), which ranges from 0 (not

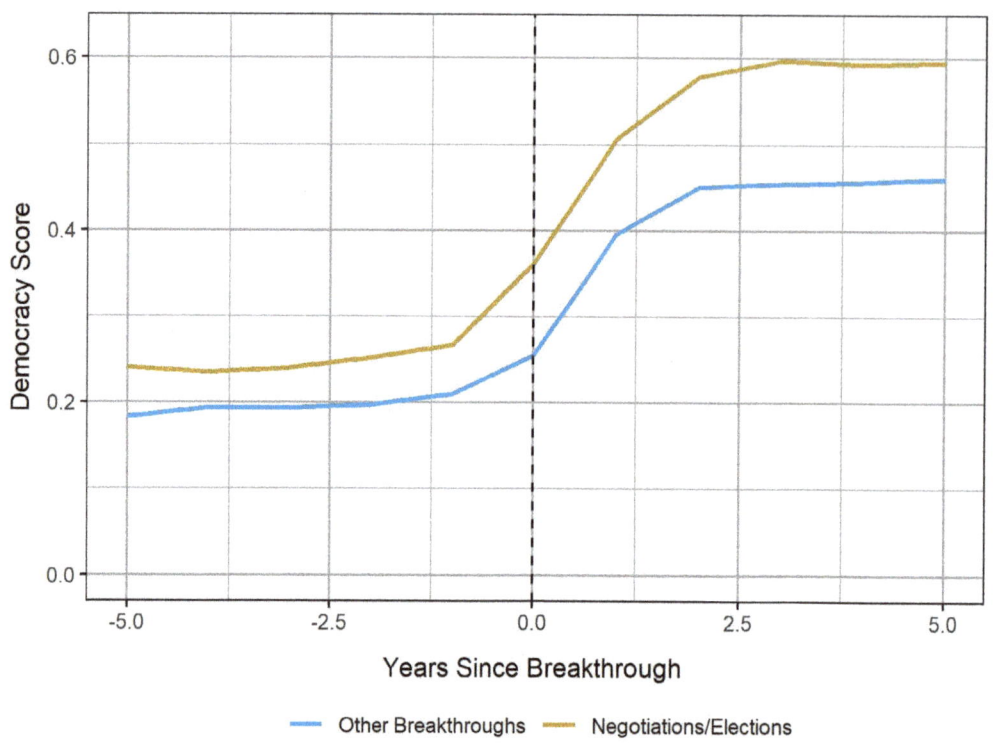

FIGURE 3: Average Levels of Democracy Across Different Breakthroughs

Source: Author calculation based on Varieties of Democracy dataset and original data collection

democratic at all) to 1 (completely democratic).[9] The countries with civil resistance-initiated elections or negotiations as their breakthroughs have levels of democracy that are roughly 0.15 higher than countries with other breakthroughs. To aid in interpretation, this difference is roughly equivalent to the difference in democracy levels between the United States and the Republic of Georgia in 2018.[10] The countries reach this difference roughly two years after the breakthrough, and it remains consistent several years into the future.

However, as **Figure 3** shows, countries that achieve breakthrough by negotiations or elections also have slightly higher levels of democracy in the years before the breakthrough, on average around 0.05 higher. While this difference is not big enough to fully account for the

---

9 Technically, the Polyarchy score measures "electoral" democracy, by combining indexes that measure whether the executive is elected, the percentage of the population that has suffrage, the freedom and fairness of elections, and the levels of protection for freedom of expression and association (Coppedge et al. 2018).

10 The Varieties of Democracy project gives the United States a score of 0.834 in 2018, and the Republic of Georgia a score of 0.676.

larger difference after breakthrough—0.15—it suggests that negotiations and elections may only arise in countries that are already more democratic, which in turn may make it easier for these countries to become stronger democracies after breakthrough.

This difference makes it crucial to analyze the effects of breakthroughs while accounting for prior levels of democracy, as well as other contextual factors that may influence a country's democratic trajectory. Breakthroughs, while significantly shaped by short-term contingent factors that may be unpredictable beforehand, are also likely to be affected by a country's long-term political and economic context—factors that also affect future levels of democracy.[11]

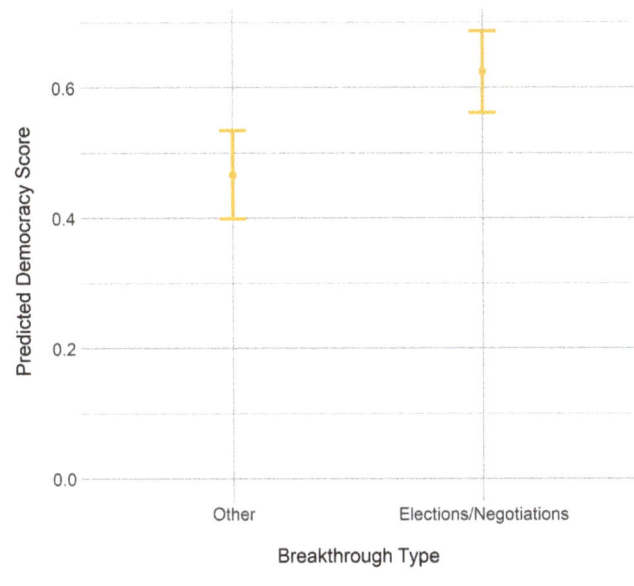

FIGURE 4: Effects of Elections/Negotiations on Democracy Five Years After Breakthrough

Source: Author calculation based on Varieties of Democracy dataset and original data collection

What is the effect of the different breakthrough mechanisms on democratization when taking the major structural factors such as the country's prior level of democracy or level of economic development into account? **Figure 4** shows the results of a statistical model[12] testing the effect of a breakthrough of negotiations or elections on the level of democracy five years after the end of a civil resistance campaign, controlling for the most common factors that have been found to influence a country's level of democracy: levels of democracy before a breakthrough, the average level of democracy in the region, and the GDP per capita.[13] The points on the graph are the predicted democracy scores five years after breakthrough for

---

11 The literature on democratization suggests a very large number of potential structural factors that might affect a country's democratic trajectory. In particular, there are strong arguments that a country's past democratic history, economic development (Acemoglu et al. 2008), and a facilitative international environment (Brinks and Coppedge 2006; Gleditsch and Ward 2006) encourage democratization.

12 The model is an OLS linear regression model. The full regression table with model fit statistics is reported in the appendix.

13 All the variables are drawn from the Varieties of Democracy project.

countries going through elections or negotiations compared to the four other breakthroughs, with all structural control variables held at their average.[14]

As **Figure 4** shows, achieving breakthrough by elections or negotiations still increases the predicted level of democracy, even when one accounts for the potential confounding effects of prior levels of democracy, economic development, and the average level of democracy in a country's region. Indeed, controlling for these factors slightly increases the predicted effect of elections and negotiations on democratization, compared to the simple average levels of democracy without controls.[15] The statistical analysis thus provides evidence that breakthroughs indeed shape the political transitions that follow them, even when taking contextual factors into account. The following section examines this impact in two recent cases.

Breakthrough by Elections in the 2018 Armenian Velvet Revolution

Events in Armenia powerfully illustrate the effects of breakthroughs by negotiations or elections on democratic progress. On April 17, 2018, the Armenian parliament elected former President Serzh Sargsyan as Armenia's prime minister. The move was widely seen as a power grab. Sargsyan had been the country's president for ten years and had overseen a constitutional revision process that changed Armenia from a presidential to a parliamentary system. This change reduced the presidency to a largely symbolic role and gave the prime minister extensive executive powers. Sargsyan had gotten approval for the change from Armenia's voters in part because he promised that in the new political dispensation he would not seek the prime ministership (Abrahamian and Shagoyan 2018).

The opposition, led by activist and Civil Contract party founder Nikol Pashinyan, initiated a weeks-long march across the country, inspired by Mohandas Gandhi's 1930 anti-tax salt march to the sea, and a series of demonstrations against Sargsyan's election (MacFarquhar 2019). Their initial protests were sparsely attended, but after Sargsyan's election, as well as the government's badly fumbled attempts at violent repression of the opposition protests, participation swelled. Opposition protesters pursued a string of innovative tactics, including flash mob road blockades that overwhelmed police capacity by quickly dispersing when officers arrived to break up the blockade but immediately reforming on a different nearby street (Amiryan n.d.).

---

[14] The bars on either side of the points are a 95% confidence interval, showing the range of reasonable variation in the predicted values. See the appendix for additional robustness checks of this relationship. The result is robust for measuring the Polyarchy score at least up to 10 years after the breakthrough.

[15] The predicted difference is roughly 0.16, compared to the roughly 0.15 difference in average scores.

While the government initially attempted violent repression, the size of the protests quickly made violence unfeasible, and the regime decided to negotiate. Pashinyan and the opposition refused to end the protests unless Sargsyan stepped down and Pashinyan was elected as prime minister. As the protests showed no signs of slowing, and the solidarity of his party began to crack under the pressure, Sargsyan eventually bowed to the protesters' demands and stepped down from power. Sargsyan's party, the Republican Party of Armenia, attempted to elect a Sargsyan loyalist to replace him, but Pashinyan refused to end the campaign until the ruling party put an opposition figure in power. Finally, on May 8, 2018, a significant number of ruling party parliamentarians defected, leading to Pashinyan's election as Prime Minister of Armenia.

The 2018 Armenian Velvet Revolution involves elements of both the resignation and election breakthroughs. The primary breakthrough mechanism was elections, as the election of Nikol Pashinyan as Armenia's Prime Minister was the primary event ending the period of struggle and initiating a transition.

The following events of the transition in Armenia illustrate the many positive effects of a "cooperative transition." First, Pashinyan's election significantly shifted the balance of power toward opposition figures. The protesters of the Velvet Revolution took full advantage of the high level of mobilization involved in the opposition to Serzh Sargsyan, not just to remove Sargsyan from power but to put a figure with more democratic preferences in a position of significant influence to shape the following transition. This paid off in the following year of transition when snap parliamentary elections held in December 2018 were deemed by independent international and national observers to be free of vote rigging or major irregularities and "contestants were able to conduct their campaigns freely; fundamental freedoms of association, assembly, expression and movement were fully respected during the campaign" (ODIHR 2019). Pashinyan was also able to use the enhanced powers of the Armenian prime ministership (which Sargsyan's constitutional reforms had empowered for his own use) to significantly reshape the Armenian polity, implement major political reforms, and begin going after corrupt officials (Ohanyan 2018).

The way the transition was set in motion in Armenia involved careful use of institutional channels. Unlike prior nonviolent revolutions in the region, such as Kyrgyzstan's Tulip Revolution (Bunce and Wolchik 2011), the leaders of the Armenian Velvet Revolution were careful to only achieve power through an undisputedly legitimate electoral process. This focus on institutions was replicated throughout the transition process, with both old regime elites and new elites carefully working whenever possible within existing legal and institutional structures (Iskandaryan 2018, 480).

The result has been a significant democratic upswing in Armenia. From 2017 to 2019, the Varieties of Democracy project has already reported a 0.4 increase in Armenia's Polyarchy score—an extremely rare and substantive increase in democracy, moving it from 121st to 35th most democratic country in the world. The new government has opened space for increased civil society activism (Liakhov and Khudoyan 2018), engaged in major anti-corruption initiatives (Atanesian 2018), and passed legislation to significantly reform the conduct of elections (Asbarez 2018). The country is still very much in transition, and the outcome remains to be determined, but many significant gains have been achieved.

Breakthrough by Coup d'État in the 2011 Egyptian Revolution

The transition in Armenia illustrates the positive democratic progress of a transition initiated through a breakthrough with a democratic balance of power, an opposition initiative, and institutionalized avenues of change. The transition in Egypt following the 2011 Arab Spring illustrates the pernicious influence of transitions initiated through a breakthrough without these characteristics, specifically the February 2011 coup d'état that ousted former President Hosni Mubarak.

In 2010, few would have predicted that major political change was on the horizon in Egypt. A nascent protest movement against President Hosni Mubarak's election to a fifth term in 2005 had been successfully snuffed out, and opposition forces were largely demobilized and demoralized. The most relevant political question was succession—who would follow the aging President Mubarak into power as his health declined?

The situation in Egypt changed dramatically when protests in Tunisia successfully ousted Tunisian President Zine El Abidine Ben Ali in January 2011. As news of the successful revolution in Tunisia spread to Egypt, increased attention was placed on a protest already planned for January 25, 2011—Egypt's "police day"—by youth activists, including the Facebook group "We are all Khaled Said"[16] organized by Egyptian Google executive Wael Ghonim. Despite violent security force repression, the protest marches on January 25 were much larger than anyone had expected and successfully reached, and briefly occupied, Cairo's symbolic Tahrir ("liberation") Square.

In the following days, opposition political parties, including the banned Muslim Brotherhood, as well as hundreds of thousands of ordinary Egyptians, joined youth protesters in Tahrir Square and around the country. After initial clashes in the first few days of protests, the police largely disappeared from Cairo's streets. The Egyptian army deployed to Cairo on January 28, 2011, but declared its intention not to interfere with the protests. The Mubarak government

---

16 Khaled Said was a young Egyptian from the city of Alexandria who was brutally tortured and murdered by Egyptian police after publicizing incidents of police brutality.

unsuccessfully attempted to demobilize the protesters through concessions, including a promise to step down after an upcoming presidential election. Protesters refused to accept these offers and demanded both Mubarak's immediate departure and action by the military to resolve the national crisis. Finally, on February 11, following an overnight meeting between Mohamed Tantawi, the Chairman of Egypt's Supreme Council of the Armed Forces (SCAF), and President Mubarak, Vice-President Omar Suleiman gave a brief statement announcing that Mubarak had stepped down and handed over political authority to Tantawi and SCAF.

Mubarak's downfall quickly received significant domestic and international acclaim. There was a sense among activists and observers that this was a genuine victory for "people power" that would usher in a quick democratic transition. The military actively encouraged this narrative, promising activists that all of their goals would be met, meeting with youth leaders such as Wael Ghonim, and forming a committee to revise the Egyptian constitution. Additionally, many of the most prominent businessmen associated with the corruption of the Mubarak regime were removed from their positions of influence and prosecuted. Yet the military remained the primary actor holding the reins of power, and its influence was never seriously threatened or controlled by any civilian institution.

The military's approach of promising major reforms while maintaining strong control over real political power demobilized much of the massive coalition that had come together to oust Mubarak. Many radical youth revolutionaries attempted to remain in Tahrir Square advocating for greater openness and democracy and condemning SCAF's authoritarian tactics. The military brutally repressed these critics. At the same time, most people either accepted the rhetoric that the army's ouster of Mubarak represented the victory of the revolution or simply no longer felt motivated to engage in political action. Organized political groups, such as the Muslim Brotherhood, split from the young revolutionaries to carve out their own political arrangement with the military.

The military arrested, detained, and tried in secret courts over 7,000 activists (Martini and Taylor 2011) within a few months of Mubarak's departure. SCAF's concern with maintaining public support and its own air of apolitical legitimacy inclined the generals to move away from direct rule, but they were determined to ensure that any future ruler would be unable to interfere with their continued political independence and domination of the country's economy. Thus, while SCAF maintained a democratic public face, its manipulation of the transition process—unchecked by any serious partner in power or institution—pushed toward keeping a non-democratic autonomous military with little or no civilian oversight or incentive to democratize.

SCAF withdrew from direct rule in 2012, with the election of Egyptian President Mohamed Morsi. Morsi's election was a moment of democratic hope. International observers hailed the election's historic nature—Egypt's first real democratic election ever. Yet optimism about

Morsi's rule dissipated in November 2012 when the president issued a constitutional declaration granting himself sweeping executive powers. After widespread protests, Morsi scrapped the declaration, but its effect was to drive away what limited opposition participation there was in the constitution-making process. This followed the completion of an Islamist-tinged constitution that was passed in a controversial low-turnout referendum.

Egypt's liberal opposition united against Morsi and began to demand his removal from power. This opposition to Morsi peaked on June 30, 2013, the first anniversary of Morsi's inauguration as president. Millions, perhaps even tens of millions, joined protests across Egypt demanding Morsi's immediate ouster. On July 3, Defence Minister Abdel Fattah el-Sisi deployed troops across Cairo and placed Morsi and much of the Muslim Brotherhood's top leadership under arrest. This was followed by a brutal military crackdown on Morsi's supporters, peaking on August 14, 2013, when the military massacred at least 600 people holding sit-ins against the coup in Cairo.

The return of brutal government repression extended beyond the Muslim Brotherhood. The military also arrested prominent youth activists and other well-known liberal opposition figures. The new Egyptian constitution, passed in a January 2014 referendum characterized by military intimidation and an opposition boycott, added *de jure* justification for this state of affairs to continue indefinitely, expanding the definition of terrorism to create a *de facto* military state, and giving the president wide powers to call a state of emergency (Revkin 2014). Defence Minister el-Sisi, after leading the coup to overthrow Egypt's only democratically elected president, quickly stepped in to replace him, winning with 97% of the vote in an election in May 2014 that all international observers denounced as far from free and fair. El-Sisi's control over the country has been cemented in subsequent years, with the evisceration of political opposition and the ever-increasing centralization of power in El-Sisi's hands.

Many factors shaped the dynamics of Egypt's chaotic transition. But the civil resistance-led breakthrough by coup in 2011 played a central role. In particular, it cemented the key position of military leaders, giving them the central position in the balance of power as the transition began. It also placed the key initiative for planning transitional arrangements in the hands of military leaders.

At each step of the subsequent transition process, the military was able to shift political outcomes toward protecting its power and privilege. Even more importantly, though, the coup of 2011 and its subsequent consolidation by the end of that year re-empowered the military and provided the template for the coup of 2013 and the full-fledged return of authoritarian rule by a military-backed president in the mold of Egypt's pre-revolutionary authoritarian regime.

Takeaways and Recommendations

This special report has presented a categorization of the ways in which civil resistance campaigns have achieved breakthroughs against non-democratic regimes over the last seventy years. It has presented evidence of the effects of these different breakthroughs on the countries' transition paths from an old, non-democratic regime to a new regime, either democratic or non-democratic.

Breakthroughs are not the only important factor that influences democratic trajectories in transitions brought about by civil resistance. Yet the statistical evidence and cases presented here provide strong reasons why policymakers, international practitioners and activists must look seriously into and take stock of the potential impact of the six breakthroughs on the transitions initiated by civil resistance movements. Breakthrough is only the first step in a transition. Yet it is a step that has an outsized impact on the steps and processes that follow it. Thus, substituting one kind of breakthrough for another may significantly change the transition pathway that follows it, inclining a country toward or away from democracy.

This work builds on the growing academic literature on the relationship between nonviolent resistance and democratization (Bayer, Bethke, and Lambach 2016; Bethke and Pinckney 2019; Celestino and Gleditsch 2013; Chenoweth and Stephan 2011; Karatnycky and Ackerman 2005). This report also provides several lessons for those involved in nonviolent resistance and for external actors interested in helping shift transitions following nonviolent resistance in a democratic direction.

Ability to shape a breakthrough is limited by history and by the political capacities of players during a civil resistance campaign. However, the report findings imply a few general guidelines for transition stakeholders, external supporters and activists alike.

1. **Increase local capacity for a democratizing breakthrough.** Achieving breakthrough via negotiations or elections can be facilitated if the relevant domestic actors have the skills and resources to pursue those avenues of change while they might also engage in civil resistance actions. An opposition with an ample capability for civil resistance but little to no capacity or skills to negotiate with a non-democratic regime or to take advantage of an electoral process opened by its civil resistance campaign will be unlikely to seek or exploit a breakthrough by these means. Instead, they will be likely to call on old political elites to come to their aid, as in Egypt, boycott or withdraw prematurely from newly established institutions calculating they can win more as outsiders, or seek an immediate disintegration of the old regime while their level of mobilization is high. These steps, however, might doom democratization efforts.

2. **Use the breakthrough to put democratizers in positions of influence.** The power of the streets is typically highest just before breakthrough occurs. Capacity to pressure old regime elites through mass action is likely to decline once breakthrough has occurred. Thus, the breakthrough moment can be a crucial time to field people with democratic and human rights credentials to elected positions and democratically minded experts to administrative structures to ensure continued influence for democratizing forces.

3. **As much as possible, establish new institutions, including procedures, norms, mechanisms and structures that facilitate democratization and protect its gains.** Changing a non-democracy to a democracy will necessarily involve significant changes in how politics is practiced. Yet activists and their external allies should be careful to quickly solidify these changes in new laws and institutions that normalize political competition. While extra-institutional political pressure is crucial to bring down a non-democratic regime, it can also be a destabilizing factor during a transition. If the breakthrough already integrates itself within new institutional procedures that can easily be translated into democratic politics, such as negotiations or elections, a potentially dangerous transitional instability can be avoided.

4. **Beware generals bearing gifts.** Coups are the most common non-cooperative breakthrough type that jeopardizes civil resistance goals, and have the worst consequences for democratic progress. They tend to elevate to positions of power regime insiders who have little interest in real democratic change.

External actors can play a role by encouraging interlocutors both in non-democratic governments and opposition movements toward cooperative transitions and breakthrough types that help initiate a transition along a more democratic pathway. The moments just before breakthrough often come with a significant amount of uncertainty, and minor thrusts in one direction or another may make a difference at a critical time. Pushes for negotiations and pluralistic elections, together with reliance on cooperative mechanisms such as dialogue and compromise, can precipitate more democratic transitions. But these should be backed up by the grassroots capacity to engage in nonviolent civil resistance actions, if needed.

As the ongoing transition in Sudan shows—to come back to the case that the report begins with—forcing a dictator to step down is only the first step in achieving democratic political change through nonviolent resistance. It is also crucial that the breakthrough leads to "winning well," setting the future on a trajectory that will push the country toward real political change.

References

Abdulshafi, *Quscondy*. 2019. Quscondy Abdulshafi—*The Nonviolent Pro-Democracy Movement in Sudan (ICNC Webinar).* **https://www.youtube.com/watch?v=eEzJ1aYQSDk** (July 6, 2019).

Abrahamian, Levon, and Gayane Shagoyan. 2018. "Velvet Revolution, Armenian Style." *Demokratizatsiya: The Journal of Post-Soviet Democratization* 26(4): 509–30.

Acemoglu, Daron, Simon Johnson, James A. Robinson, and Pierre Yard. 2008. "Income and Democracy." *American Economic Review* 98(3): 808-42.

Ackerman, Peter, and Jack DuVall. 2000. *A Force More Powerful: A Century of Non-Violent Conflict.* London, UK: Palgrave Macmillan.

Amiryan, Tigran. "Culture of Protest: The Symbols of Armenia's Velvet Revolution." *The Calvert Journal.* **https://www.calvertjournal.com/articles/show/10318/culture-of-protest-symbols-of-armenia-velvet-revolution** (January 1, 2019).

Asbarez. 2018. "International Observers Urge Continued Electoral Reforms in Armenia." *Asbarez.com.* **http://asbarez.com/176630/international-observers-urge-continued-electoral-reforms-in-armenia/** (July 8, 2019).

Atanesian, Grigor. 2018. "Armenia: Anti-Corruption Purge." *LobeLog.* **https://lobelog.com/armenia-anti-corruption-purge/** (July 8, 2019).

Bayer, Markus, Felix S. Bethke, and Daniel Lambach. 2016. "The Democratic Dividend of Nonviolent Resistance." *Journal of Peace Research* 53(6): 758-771.

Bethke, Felix S., and Jonathan Pinckney. 2019. "Nonviolent Resistance and the Quality of Democracy." *Conflict Management and Peace Science* Onlinefirst **https://doi.org/10.1177/0738894219855918**.

Brinks, Daniel, and Michael Coppedge. 2006. "Diffusion Is No Illusion: Neighbor Emulation in the Third Wave of Democracy." *Comparative Political Studies* 39(4): 463-489.

Bunce, Valerie J., and Sharon L. Wolchik. 2011. *Defeating Authoritarian Leaders in Postcommunist Countries.* New York, NY: Cambridge University Press.

Butcher, Charles R., John L. Gray, and Liesel Mitchell. 2018. "Striking It Free? Organized Labor and the Outcomes of Civil Resistance." *Journal of Global Security Studies* 3(3): 302-321.

Celestino, Mauricio Rivera, and Kristian Skrede Gleditsch. 2013. "Fresh Carnations or All Thorn, No Rose? Nonviolent Campaigns and Transitions in Autocracies." *Journal of Peace Research* 50(3): 385-400.

Chenoweth, Erica, and Orion A. Lewis. 2013. "Unpacking Nonviolent Campaigns: Introducing the NAVCO 2.0 Dataset." *Journal of Peace Research* 50(3): 415-423.

Chenoweth, Erica, and Maria J. Stephan. 2011. *Why Civil Resistance Works: The Strategic Logic of Nonviolent Conflict.* New York, NY: Columbia University Press.

Coppedge, Michael et al. 2018. *V-Dem Country-Year Dataset V8.* Gothenburg, Sweden: Varieties of Democracy (V-Dem) Project.

Dudouet, Véronique. 2008. *Nonviolent Resistance and Conflict Transformation in Power Asymmetries*. Berlin, Germany: Berghof Research Center for Constructive Conflict Management.

Fernandes, Tiago. 2015. "Rethinking Pathways to Democracy: Civil Society in Portugal and Spain, 1960s-2000s." *Democratization* 22(6): 1074-1104.

Geddes, Barbara, Joseph Wright, and Erica Frantz. 2014. "Autocratic Breakdown and Regime Transitions: A New Data Set." *Perspectives on Politics* 12(2): 313-331.

Gleditsch, Kristian Skrede, and Michael D. Ward. 2006. "Diffusion and the International Context of Democratization." *International organization* 60(4): 911-933.

Helvey, Robert L. 2004. *On Strategic Nonviolent Conflict: Thinking about the Fundamentals*. Albert Einstein Institute.

Iskandaryan, Alexander. 2018. "The Velvet Revolution in Armenia: How to Lose Power in Two Weeks." *Demokratizatsiya: The Journal of Post-Soviet Democratization* 26(4): 465-82.

Karatnycky, Adrian, and Peter Ackerman. 2005. *How Freedom Is Won: From Civic Resistance to Durable Democracy*. Washington, DC: Freedom House.

Lakey, George. 2011. "The Global Nonviolent Action Database." **https://nvdatabase.swarthmore.edu/** (June 11, 2019).

Liakhov, Peter, and Knar Khudoyan. 2018. "How Citizens Battling a Controversial Gold Mining Project Are Testing Armenia's New Democracy." *openDemocracy*. **https://www.opendemocracy.net/en/odr/citizens-battling-a-controversial-gold-mining-project-amulsar-armenia/** (January 18, 2019).

MacFarquhar, Neil. 2019. "He Was a Protester a Month Ago. Now, Nikol Pashinyan Leads Armenia." *The New York Times*. **https://www.nytimes.com/2018/05/08/world/europe/armenia-nikol-pashinyan-prime-minister.html**.

Madestam, Andreas, Daniel Shoag, Stan Veuger, and David Yanagizawa-Drott. 2013. "Do Political Protests Matter? Evidence from the Tea Party Movement." *Quarterly Journal of Economics* 128(4): 1633-85.

Martini, Jeff, and Julie Taylor. 2011. "Commanding Democracy in Egypt: The Military's Attempt to Manage the Future." *Foreign Aff.* 90: 127.

Nepstad, Sharon Erickson. 2011. *Nonviolent Revolutions: Civil Resistance in the Late 20th Century*. New York, NY: Oxford University Press.

———. 2015. *Nonviolent Struggle: Theories, Strategies, and Dynamics*. New York, NY: Oxford University Press.

ODIHR. 2019. *Republic of Armenia Early Parliamentary Elections 9 December 2018: ODIHR Election Observation Mission Final Report*. OSCE Office for Democratic Institutions and Human Rights. **https://www.osce.org/odihr/elections/armenia/413555?download=true**.

O'Donnell, Guillermo, and Philippe C. Schmitter. 1986. *Transitions from Authoritarian Rule: Tentative Conclusions about Uncertain Democracies*. Baltimore, MD: JHU Press.

Ohanyan, Anna. 2018. "Armenia's Democratic Dreams." *Foreign Policy*. **https://foreignpolicy.com/2018/11/07/armenias-democratic-dreams/** (January 1, 2019).

Pinckney, Jonathan. 2014. *Winning Well: Civil Resistance Mechanisms of Success, Democracy, and Civil Peace*. Denver, CO: University of Denver (M.A. Thesis).

———. 2018. *When Civil Resistance Succeeds: Building Democracy After Popular Nonviolent Uprisings*. Washington, DC: ICNC Press.

Revkin, Mara. 2014. "Worse Than Mubarak." *Foreign Affairs*.

Schock, Kurt. 2005. *Unarmed Insurrections: People Power Movements in Nondemocracies*. Minneapolis, MN: U of Minnesota Press.

Sharp, Gene. 1973. *The Politics of Nonviolent Action*. Boston, MA: Porter Sargent.

———. 2005. *Waging Nonviolent Struggle: 20th Century Practice and 21st Century Potential*. Boston, MA: Porter Sargent.

Stephan, Maria J., and Erica Chenoweth. 2008. "Why Civil Resistance Works: The Strategic Logic of Nonviolent Conflict." *International Security* 33(1): 7-44.

Svensson, Isak, and Magnus Lundgren. 2018. "From Revolution to Resolution: Exploring Third-Party Mediation in Nonviolent Uprisings." *Peace & Change* 43(3): 271-91.

Wanis-St. John, Anthony, and Noah Rosen. 2017. *Negotiating Civil Resistance*. Washington, DC: United States Institute of Peace. **https://www.usip.org/sites/default/files/2017-07/pw129-negotiating-civil-resistance.pdf**.

Wasow, Omar. 2017. "Do Protests Matter? Evidence from the 1960s Black Insurgency." *Working Paper*: 63.

APPENDIX

Coding Rules for Determining Breakthrough Type

Coding the breakthrough type for successful civil resistance campaigns involved significant independent research, to establish both the sequence of events at the conclusion of the civil resistance campaign and the specific events that most accurately capture the moment of breakthrough. This research process primarily relied on scholarly accounts of the cases in question, though some recent cases were supplemented with newspaper or other media accounts.

In most cases, the determination of the breakthrough type was straightforward, as scholarly sources and media accounts agreed on the sequence of events leading to the campaign's success. However, in some cases the coding process required the exercise of judgment between plausible alternatives. Because of the specificity and complexity of the cases, it was not practical to formulate hard rules for determining between these alternatives, beyond the general rule of choosing the alternative that best captured the sequence of political events that most directly precipitated the initiation of the political transition. Determinations had to be made on a case-by-case basis.

Because of the contingency of this process, each coding decision was carefully sourced and documented, with detailed methodological notes outlining the case-by-case logic for choosing one breakthrough type over another. Two examples of these are presented below for illustrative purposes.

Example Breakthrough Type Coding Determinations

Name: South African Defiance Campaign
Country: South Africa
End Year: 1992
Transition Mechanism: Negotiation

Summary: A series of nonviolent mass uprisings, including boycotts of white businesses, creation of alternative institutions, and labor strikes, as well as an international divestment and sanctions campaign, led the government of apartheid South Africa to engage in a negotiated transition process, under the auspices of the Convention for a Democratic South Africa (CODESA). While it faced significant challenges, CODESA eventually led to an agreement in late 1992 to hold national elections and a five-year national unity government. The election, held in 1994, led to the election of freedom fighter Nelson Mandela as South Africa's first black president.

Methodological Note: South Africa's transition presents a significant coding challenge. There are three significant points which can be argued as the mechanism of success: President de Klerk's decision to legalize the African National Congress (ANC) and free Nelson Mandela in 1990, the CODESA negotiations which concluded in 1992, and the election in 1994. CODESA negotiations is the best choice for the following reasons:

- The 1990 decisions by de Klerk—while they significantly increased the ability of the ANC to shape the future of South Africa—did not lead to a real shift in power, thus they are not significant enough to be considered the mechanism of transition.

- The 1994 election, while groundbreaking, took place under an already agreed upon negotiated framework. When the election took place, the ANC was already in the position of strenuously pushing its agenda that built on its formidable political influence and was guaranteed at least some role in the post-election government (because of the agreements on forming a government of national unity made at CODESA). The election thus determined primarily how big the ANC's power in the government would be, not whether they would have a role.

- The negotiated agreement from CODESA thus represents the best coding of the transition mechanism. It gave the ANC and other African groups significant political influence, and critically shaped how South Africa's future transition took place.

Sources:
Davenport, T.R.H. *The Birth of a New South Africa.* Toronto, Canada: University of Toronto Press (1998).

Jackson, John. "The 1994 Election: An Analysis." In F.H. Toase and E.J. Yorke (eds.) *The New South Africa: Prospects for Domestic and International Security.* New York, NY: St. Martin's Press (1998).

Schock, Kurt. *Unarmed Insurrections: People Power Movements in Nondemocracies.* Minneapolis, MN: University of Minnesota Press (2005).

Name: Bulldozer Revolution/Otpor
Country: Yugoslavia
End Year: 2000
Transition Mechanism: Election

Summary: The Serbian student movement Otpor spearheaded a campaign of civil resistance against Serbian dictator Slobodan Milošević, engaging in creative protests to undermine the narrative of Milosevic's inevitable rule and successfully unifying the fragmented Serbian opposition into the Democratic Opposition of Serbia (DOS). Due in large part to Otpor's efforts, DOS's presidential candidate, Vojislav Koštunica, defeated Milošević in the 2000 Yugoslavian presidential election. When Milošević falsely claimed that Koštunica had received less than 50% of the vote, and thus a second round of elections was called for, Otpor and opposition activists engaged in a wave of massive demonstrations occupying central Belgrade, while outside of Belgrade workers at the Kolubara coal mines (which supplied half of the country's electricity) went on strike. Faced with increasing resistance and with police largely refusing to obey orders to disperse protesters, the constitutional court reversed its ruling requiring a second round of elections. Subsequently, Milošević renounced his claim to the presidency, and Kostunica was made President of Yugoslavia.

Methodological Note: Coding the transition mechanism in this case is challenging because of different possible interpretations of the importance of the election. An argument could be made for this case being an example of negotiation (because the court reversed its decision and Milošević stepped down after meetings with Koštunica), or of overwhelming (since after the election, the massive protests, strikes, and defections by police and local government officials were crucial in ending Milošević's rule). However, while the largest mobilization took place after the election itself, I consider the election to be the crucial transition mechanism for a number of reasons:

- Winning the election was clearly a necessary component for the mobilization which took place afterwards.

- The protests were explicitly focused on ensuring the government honored the terms of the election rather than seeking a different route to power, e.g. through negotiation or extra-institutional seizure of power.

- The final victory took the form of the constitutional court reversing its stand on the second round of elections and Milosevic acknowledging the results of the first round of elections.

Sources:
Bunce, Valerie J. and Sharon L. Wolchik. *Defeating Authoritarian Leaders in Postcommunist Countries.* Cambridge, England: Cambridge University Press.

Rennebohm, Max. "Serbians Overthrow Milosevic (Bulldozer Revolution), 2000." *Global Nonviolent Action Database* (2011, September 8). Accessed 12/12/13 at **http://nvdatabase.swarthmore.edu/content/serbians-overthrow-milosevic-bulldozer-revolution-2000**.

Tucker, Joshua A. "Enough! Electoral Fraud, Collective Action Problems, and Postcommunist Colored Revolutions." *Perspectives on Politics* 5, no. 3 (2007): 535-551.

TABLE A1: Complete List of Cases with Breakthrough Types

Nonviolent Action campaigns come primarily from NAVCO 1.1 and NAVCO 2.0. Breakthrough type is based on original author research.

COUNTRY	YEAR	CAMPAIGN NAME	BREAKTHROUGH TYPE
Guatemala	1945	October Revolutionaries	Coup
India	1947	Gandhian Campaign	Negotiation
Haiti	1956		Resignation
Ghana	1957	Convention People's Party movement	Election
Colombia	1958	Anti-Rojas	Coup
Venezuela	1958	Anti-Jimenez	Coup
Democratic Republic of Congo	1960		Negotiation
South Korea	1960	South Korea Student Revolution	Resignation
Dominican Republic	1962	Anti-Balaguer	Coup
Zambia	1964	Zambia Anti-occupation	Election
Malawi	1964	Nyasaland African Congress	Negotiation
Sudan	1965		Negotiation
Madagascar	1972	Anti-Tsiranana Campaign	Resignation
Thailand	1973	Thai student protests	Coup
Portugal	1974	Carnation Revolution	Coup
Greece	1974	Greece Anti-Military	Coup
Bolivia	1979	Bolivian Anti-Junta	Resignation
Iran	1979	Iranian Revolution	Overwhelming
Bolivia	1982	Bolivian Anti-Junta	Negotiation
Argentina	1983	Argentina pro-democracy movement	Election
Uruguay	1984	Uruguay Anti-Military	Election
Brazil	1985	Diretas Ja	Election
Sudan	1985	Anti-Jaafar	Coup
Haiti	1986	Anti-Duvalier	Resignation
Philippines	1986	People Power	Overwhelming
South Korea	1987	South Korea Anti-Military	Election
Panama	1989	Anti-Noriega	Foreign Intervention
Chile	1989	Anti-Pinochet Movement	Election
East Germany	1989	East Germany pro-dem movement	Resignation
Poland	1989	Solidarity	Negotiation
Czechoslovakia	1989	Velvet Revolution	Negotiation
Hungary	1990	Hungary pro-dem movement	Negotiation
Bulgaria	1990	Bulgaria Anti-Communist	Negotiation
Benin	1990	Benin Anti-Communist	Negotiation
Mongolia	1990	Mongolian Anti-communist	Resignation

COUNTRY	YEAR	CAMPAIGN NAME	BREAKTHROUGH TYPE
Bangladesh	1990	Bangladesh Anti-Ershad	Resignation
Nepal	1990	The Stir	Negotiation
Albania	1991	Albania Anti-Communist	Resignation
Slovenia	1991	Slovenian Independence	Election
Soviet Union	1991	Russia pro-dem movement	Overwhelming
Estonia	1991	Singing Revolution	Election
Latvia	1991	Latvia pro-dem movement	Election
Lithuania	1991	Sajudis/ Lithuanian pro-democracy movement	Election
Belarus	1991	Belarus Anti-Communist	Coup
Georgia	1991	Georgia Anti-Soviet	Election
Mali	1991	Mali Anti-Military	Coup
Niger	1991	Niger Anti-Military	Negotiation
Zambia	1991	Zambia Anti-Single Party	Election
Guyana	1992	Anti-Burnham/Hoyte	Election
Thailand	1992	Thai pro-dem movement	Election
Nigeria	1993	Nigeria Anti-Military	Resignation
Central African Republic	1993		Election
Madagascar	1993	Active Forces	Negotiation
Malawi	1994	Anti-Banda	Election
South Africa	1994	South Africa Second Defiance Campaign	Negotiation
Nigeria	1999	Nigeria Anti-Military	Election
Indonesia	1999	Anti-Suharto	Resignation
Mexico	2000	Anti-PRI	Election
Peru	2000	Anti-Fujimori	Resignation
Croatia	2000	Croatian Institutional Reform	Election
Serbia	2000	Anti-Milosevic	Election
Senegal	2000	Anti-Diouf	Election
Ghana	2000		Election
Lesotho	2002		Election
Madagascar	2002	Madagascar pro-democracy movement	Negotiation
East Timor	2002		Foreign Intervention
Georgia	2003	Rose Revolution	Resignation
Ukraine	2004	Orange Revolution	Election
Lebanon	2005	Cedar Revolution	Resignation
Kyrgyzstan	2005	Tulip Revolution	Overwhelming
Liberia	2003	Women of Liberia Mass Action for Peace	Foreign Intervention
Nepal	2006	Nepalese Anti-government	Election
Pakistan	2008	Lawyer's Movement	Resignation
Tunisia	2011	Anti-Ben Ali Campaign (Jasmine Revolution)	Resignation
Egypt	2011	Anti-Mubarak Movement	Coup
Yemen	2011	Anti-Saleh Movement	Negotiation

This section presents the full regression tables for the model output presented in **Figure 4**, which has been generated using the predicted values from Model 2 (the model including control variables).

TABLE A2: Full OLS Model Regression Table and Robustness Check Results

Author calculation based on original data collection

EFFECT OF ELECTIONS OR NEGOTIATIONS ON POST-TRANSITION DEMOCRACY		
	DEPENDENT VARIABLE	
	Polyarchy Score t + 5	
	(1)	(2)
Election or Negotiation Breakthrough	0.115** (0.053)	0.157*** (0.047)
Pre-Breakthrough Polyarchy		-0.098 (0.188)
Average Regional Democracy		0.306*** (0.112)
GDP per capita (log)		0.071*** (0.026)
Constant	0.480*** (0.039)	-0.179 (0.218)
Observations	76	68
R2	0.060	0.363
Adjusted R2	0.047	0.323
Residual Std. Error	0.230 (df = 74)	0.186 (df = 63)
F Statistic	4.716** (df = 1; 74)	8.981*** (df = 4; 63)
Note:	* p < 0.1, ** p < 0.05, *** p < 0.01	

The complete replication data files, including all analysis files and the complete set of methodological notes and sources for the coding of individual cases are available from the author upon request. Contact Jonathan Pinckney via email at **jpinckney@usip.org** or at **www.jonathanpinckney.com**.

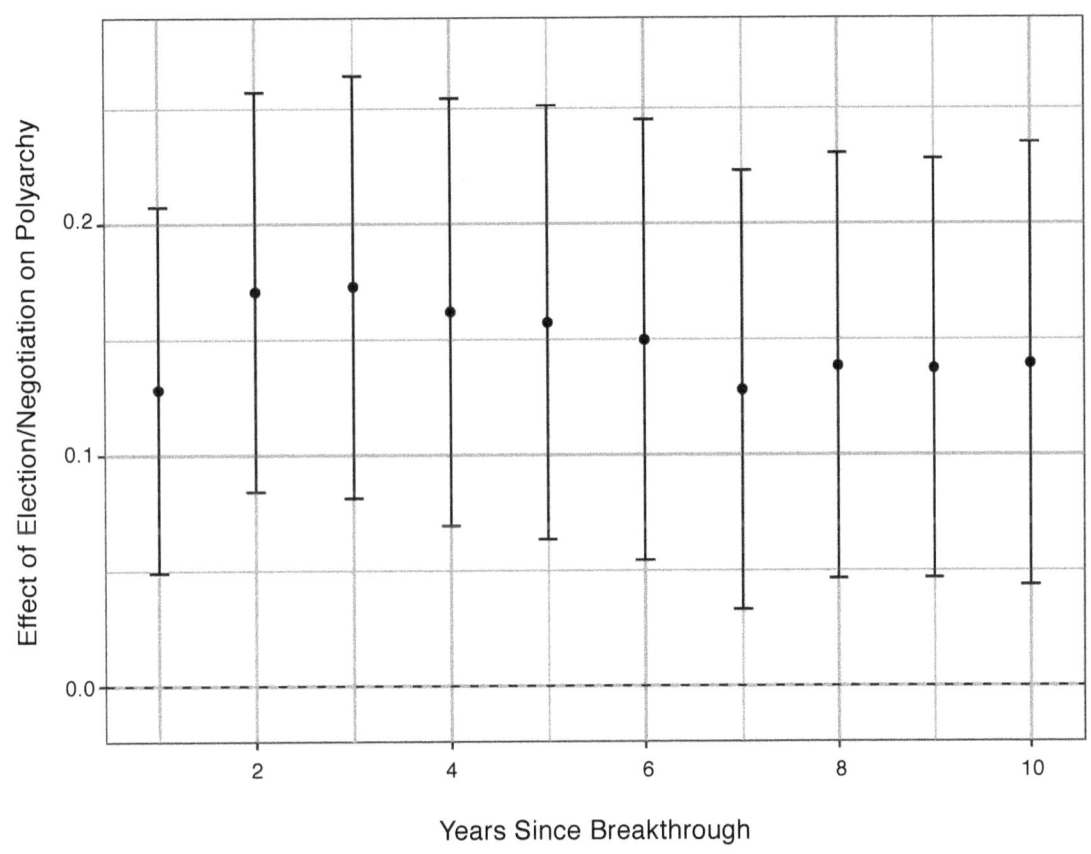

FIGURE A1: Primary Model Robustness Checks (t + 1 to t + 10)

Author calculation based on Varieties of Democracy dataset

Figure A1 shows a coefficient plot of separate models measuring the impact of achieving breakthrough via negotiations or elections on the level of democracy from time *t + 1* through *t + 10*. The individual points are the coefficients, while the lines enclose a 95% confidence interval. There is a horizontal dashed line at zero. Coefficients whose lower bound of the confidence interval do not cross the zero line are significant at a $p < 0.05$ level. Each point is from a separate model using the same set of controls from Model 2 in Table A2 and measuring the polyarchy score at the indicated number of years out from the breakthrough. Since the independent variable is binary (coded as a one if the breakthrough type was a negotiation or election and as a zero otherwise), the coefficient is equal to the marginal effect of these breakthrough types on future polyarchy scores. The results indicate that the effect of breakthrough types is robust for the entire decade following the initial breakthrough.

About the Author

Jonathan Pinckney is a Program Officer with the Program on Nonviolent Action at the United States Institute of Peace, where he conducts research on nonviolent action, peacebuilding, and democratization. He is the author of the book *From Dissent to Democracy: The Promise and Peril of Civil Resistance Transitions*, from Oxford University Press, as well as a wide range of academic and general audience publications. He received his PhD in 2018 from the University of Denver. He was a 2012 recipient of the Sie Cheou-Kang Fellowship at the University of Denver, and a 2016 recipient of an ICNC PhD Fellowship. The opinions in this piece are solely those of the author and do not necessarily reflect the opinions of the United States Institute of Peace.